THE SILVER LINK LIBRARY OF
RAILWAY MODELLING
●
CREATIVE
SCENIC MODELLING

THE SILVER LINK LIBRARY OF RAILWAY MODELLING

●

CREATIVE SCENIC MODELLING

A PRACTICAL APPROACH TO MODEL RAILWAY LANDSCAPING

John Parkinson

SLP

Silver Link Publishing Ltd

First published in 2010

British Library Cataloguing in Publication Data

A catalogue record for this book is available from the British Library.

ISBN 978 1 85794 352 8

Silver Link Publishing Ltd
The Trundle
Ringstead Road
Great Addington
Kettering
Northants NN14 4BW

Tel/Fax: 01536 330588
email: sales@nostalgiacollection.com
Website: www.nostalgiacollection.com

Printed and bound in the Czech Republic

All photographs are by the author

Title page **A general view of the author's 'Porth Kernow' 'N' gauge layout.**

A Silver Link book
from
The NOSTALGIA *Collection*

ACKNOWLEDGEMENTS

A big thank you to my son-in-law Gareth and son Jack who put the words and pictures of the first version of this manuscript together so well, and Tim Taylor who worked initially on the text and scanned old photos. Thanks also to my family and friends for their encouragement and support: to my wife Chris, my brother Steve, daughters Nancy, Frances, Ruth and Bridget, son-in-law Haco, daughter-in-law Karen, Lee, Paul, John Gunton, and helpers at shows, including Dave McIver ('The Thin Controller'), Gerry Baker and Chris Fosbury, Jack and Andy Cooper, Paul, Rhys, Jaimie and others.

Thanks also to my friends and colleagues from model railway clubs and groups, notably Tring (Peter and Joan Jay, Mike Upton, Don Pearson, Derek Town and Mike Sumpter), Southport (Tony Kuivala, Peter Mills and Bill Gates), and Porthmadog (Paul Towers, Vaughan Jones, Barry Lindsey, Alun Roberts, et al), Julie Williams and the staff of Llanberis slate museum, Bill Newton and all at the Corris Railway, not forgetting model railway magazine editors who have encouraged me and published so many of my articles, especially Andrew Burnham. You have all helped me to believe in the value of what for me has always been a labour of love.

Thanks also to Will Adams and Mick Sanders for their editorial and design skills on behalf of Silver Link Publishing Ltd.

Finally I would like to dedicate this book to the memory of young Lisa, whose loss made me even more determined to continue on this creative journey.

CONTENTS

INTRODUCTION

I'm what I believe the Americans call a 'scenery nut', and as well as appealing to those of like mind, I'm also keen to gain a few converts, especially those among you who feel that scenic modelling is beyond you, and even more especially the younger enthusiast, of whom there are sadly all too few at the present time.

I know there are some of you out there whose interest centres mainly round trains, and especially steam engines, and of course there's nothing wrong with that. (Dare I say it – in traction terms, it's diesels that turn me on!) You'll forgive me I hope if I declare my bias right from the start, together with the hope that after reading this book a few more of you will be keen on developing your modelling skills. In essence, what I want to show you is how I get from the pictures on page 8 to those on page 9, as well as making buildings and structures to create an integrated scene. I want essentially to try and provide in words and pictures an overview of my modelling, which involves in the first instance a look at how it developed, with a brief survey of some of my earlier creations, before I get to the details of my current layouts, hopefully showing that if I can do it, so can you. (If you already have, then at the very least you can compare notes!)

I would like to make it clear at the outset that I have attempted to justify my writing of this book by convincing myself that I am a modeller whose efforts can be equalled or surpassed by most people if they really want to. I am well aware that there are quite a number of better modellers than me; initially I felt inadequate by comparison, but shrugged it off and got on anyway, and that's what I hope you'll do or are doing. It's good to be inspired by other people's creations, but not if it makes you feel you can't possibly emulate them.

In my case, as my mother would have told you all too readily, and to my minor embarrassment, from an early age I exhibited an interest in making things out of card and paper (the infamous examples being 'monkey houses', the monkeys sadly only two-dimensional). Even now I must confess to a certain thrill of anticipation as I sit down at my table to create something new, still mostly from card.

In essence, what I'm setting out to do in this book is to seek to convey to you something of my love of creative scenic modelling, and hopefully inspire you to do something similar. Of course everybody is different, and that's how it should be. If you haven't already, you will want to develop your own style and way of doing things. Although I've been modelling for 30 years, I still eagerly read books and magazines, looking to pick up ideas and tips, trying out new methods where possible.

There will be those of you who have plenty of experience of your own, and will know ways of doing the things I'm going to describe that are just as good or even better (and I hope I will meet you some time to discuss them, if I haven't already!). Others will be grappling with the basic concepts of scenery contours or structure modelling, and looking for ways to develop further. And there will be those of you who have seen models or layouts at an exhibition or in a magazine, and are wondering where to begin.

I'm hoping to provide something of interest for all of you. Inevitably, there will be bits of what I write that the more experienced of you can simply gloss over, and hopefully not think me condescending in the process – like possibly what I'm going to say now, which applies to those starting out, like the people I talk to at shows, some of whom only went to accompany their spouse or other family members and friends, but then had a pleasant surprise in finding that there

The scenery contours for the hills, estuary and farm on 'Caer Faban' (*this page*), and the completed scenes (*opposite*).

was more than track and trains on show, and had a glimpse of the potential of scenic modelling.

You don't need great expertise to be a successful scenic modeller – it's not rocket science! I make baseboards, lay track and wire up electric points, but I'm not an expert at these things – I want to say I did it myself, and enjoy the satisfaction that brings. However, mainly I want to get on with making the scenery and structures, because that's what really motivates me. Neither do I consider myself as having any special gift for scenic modelling; my achievements are based mainly on enthusiasm, and practice. You've got to want to do it – if you do, you'll find the time, and the necessary patience, maybe in small bursts, because of temporary setbacks or other commitments, but you'll get there in the end. I'm fortunate that, now I'm retired, I'm 'time-rich', but it wasn't always so. For years I was a teacher and foster-parent, and (with the help of my wife!) brought up five children. At that time I had a layout in the attic, which I got on with making in odd half-hours, or occasional longer stretches of free time. But I finished each stage of a project in the end. I have no particular practical skills, but I have an urge to be creative, to develop a three-dimensional picture of some scene or combination of scenes.

I hear people say, 'I've tried, but it just didn't work for me.' Well, I've lost count of the number of times I've scrapped half-finished structures, or remade sections of scenery, or not got my edges square on window frames, or used the wrong glue or painted things an unsuitable shade – all these things still happen to me today, though perhaps less frequently, and I could point to lots of things on my models that I think could be better. But what matters in the end is that you want to make a scene that gels, looks like a composite whole, and has atmosphere. That's what I'm aiming for all the time, whether I'm working from American, British or German prototypes, in either 'OO' or 'N' gauge.

If you just want a train (or lots of trains), an engine shed, some fencing and a few lineside effects, or even a shunting yard, so that your layout doesn't look rather like a test track, this book is probably not for you. If, on the other hand, your aim is to create a scene that the trains merely complete, but could stand on its own merits even if there was no railway component at all, then

read on! (In practice, of course, running trains is very desirable, very popular with children and like-minded adults, and essential if you want to get invited to model railway exhibitions!)

Recently I saw a home layout with lots of scenery and structures, mostly well made (admittedly some of the houses were made from kits, but that's fine if you don't want to scratchbuild). But what struck me immediately was that, though the individual components were quite well done, the scene as a whole did not look right, and on closer inspection I could see why. (I must stress that this is constructive criticism, pointing out how you can be more effective in your planning and execution.) It was too cluttered, with every available space filled with buildings, roads, a cricket pitch, canal, harbour and, of course, railway lines. The impression given was that the creator was thinking, 'How many buildings and features can I fit into this space?' There were therefore square edges and small gaps between roads, tracks and houses, with vertical dividers disguised as walls – just the way I used to be myself! Now, however, although I make small scenes, I hope that I manage to give the impression that they are natural, and the whole looks like a slice of countryside with buildings, even though I am in fact putting in more than you would really get in that given scale space.

I make just about all of my scenery and structures myself, because that's what I think gives my layouts their uniqueness. But it's only fair to point out that today (as opposed to even ten years ago) there is an enormous variety of proprietary models and materials available, all of which make life a lot easier for the scenic modeller. It's really a question of how much you want to do yourself. Like most people, I use lots of scenic materials, and am very happy to do so. It's just a question of drawing a line between what you make and what you buy ready-made, which in some cases is not a clear line, such as with tree kits, where you might buy the components but assemble and paint them yourself. And I do buy (often already painted!) signals, some fencing, telegraph poles, window glazing, plastic card and even ready-made trees, just to mention a few items, which I think enhance a scene without detracting from its originality. As I have already indicated, I am not aiming for perfection!

You may be aware of modellers who have worked

at scenes for years, and achieved what amounts to perfection. I know of a few myself, and even number one or two among my own acquaintances, but while I admire their work I wouldn't even try to emulate them, because I don't think I've got the skill, let alone the patience and endurance. In being aware of my own limitations, I'm hoping to avoid giving you the impression that what I have done is not achievable – quite the opposite.

Moreover, I am looking to be creative on a smaller scale. Today I model in the smaller scales (mainly N gauge, 2mm to the foot, or 1/148-160, but also 'OO' gauge, 4mm to the foot, or 1/76). Also I only make small scenes, what amounts to working dioramas or layout 'cameos'. This is because I have realised that it is better to have on the go a project that is capable of completion, which you can see evolving and you will finish before it finishes you!

In essence, I believe that small is beautiful – something manageable, which allows you to concentrate your efforts towards getting that quality finish that speaks for itself in its impact on the viewer, without having spent a lifetime to achieve it. If you start out with grandiose plans, you may well overreach yourself, and never complete your project.

Small layouts are also practical, will fit into your car, can go with you if you move house and, in case you think you can improve on them, enable you to start afresh next time! And you can choose a different subject to model, so you get variety, which as everybody knows is…!

After this brief introduction to set the scene, I would now like to go into more detail on how I have got to the stage I'm at today, then move on to how I actually make the models and scenery you see in the pictures.

The railbus leaving the station halt on my German-outline layout 'Der Nordseehafen'.

A DMU emerges from the tunnel on my 1991 'Bodarfryn' layout.

1
EARLY DAYS: EXPERIENCES IN 'OO'

Before I get on to the basics of scenic modelling, I'd like first to say a little bit about how I came to be where I am now. I don't mean a retiree in Blaenau Ffestiniog, though that is not completely irrelevant, as Snowdonia scenery has been a big source of inspiration for me – I am of course referring to the stage of modelling I'm at (no facetious comments are required at this juncture!).

As is quite often the case, the impetus for me to take up railway modelling was the arrival of our own children. As a child myself, I had shared a baseboard with my brother, and for a while we ran trains, but never got to the stage of making scenery. When my son Jack was 3, he got an 'OO'

train set for Christmas, and I built a baseboard for it. I also progressed to making some simple hills out of plaster, soon scrapped as very heavy and messy. But Jack was never very enthusiastic, and when he got his first computer (although in the early 1980s they were still very basic) he lost interest altogether. However, I then started building card kits and making simple fields and roads, but on a flat board.

After a year or two we moved to a big old house in Snowdonia with an attic, and I built a layout round one of the two attic rooms, even with some contours for hills and a river bed. I spent hours making station platforms, my first scratchbuilt houses, and even a cricket ground (yes, I'm keen

The cricket ground.

on that too!). In positive moments I thought I was getting somewhere, but after I'd bought and read Barry Norman's *Landscape Modelling* I knew I had to reassess my techniques!

It was then – and this is the main point, with salutary lessons for us all, me included – that I realised I hadn't been doing the basics right. (Some of you may recognise the plot of this story!) By basics I don't just, or even primarily, mean the baseboard (although I have developed my style for that too – see Chapter 2). I mean the way you go about your scenery, starting from the prototype right through to the way you design the scenery contours and complete the detailing. Also, I was trying to cram too many features into too small a space (the cricket ground for example!). The result of my new application of these concepts was 'Bodarfryn', a picture of which appeared on the front cover of *Model Railway Enthusiast*, though even then I still had not developed the sense of fine detailing to the degree I have now.

In a sense I wasted a few years, because I was not following what are in essence very simple rules. This was reinforced later when I came to look at, and eventually seek to emulate, American styles of modelling as described by Dave Frary in his book *How to Build Realistic Model Railroad Scenery*.

Of course, I will be going into these 'basics' in more detail in the following chapters, but essentially they revolve round using water-based materials both for the hard shell of the scenery contours and the painting and texturing, and also the scratchbuilding techniques you use, which in my case is mainly with card of various thicknesses, matchwood, and some plastic sheet. But I will also seek to indicate that elusive and indeterminate 'X factor' in how you put things together to get the final effect, which people say makes my layouts particularly effective. The trouble is, I'm not sure that I can analyse it myself! Obviously, photos are usually more revealing than words, and videos have been suggested, but I'm pretty slow, so that's impractical, and it's not easy to keep stopping to photograph stages of construction, though I do this with some models, and I have got some photos to show how I develop the basic scenery.

As you will probably already know, there are several different ways of doing most things, and basic scenic modelling is no exception. There are also many different techniques for building structures, and an almost bewildering variety of materials for most items, small or large.

In describing the methods and materials I have chosen, I may have developed some originality and personal style, but I am not claiming to have invented essentially new techniques and, as I already have, I will continue to refer to people and articles that have inspired me.

What I am trying to present is an insight into one individual's modelling world, which I hope will encourage you to believe that you in your own way can do exactly the same kind of thing, and quite possibly to greater effect.

I've decided to start the more detailed look at my modelling by covering the time I spent 'working' (it's all fun really!) in 'OO' scale, as that was my next chronological stage, and it forms a natural progression in my development. It was during this period that I made my momentous decision to re-examine my basic techniques, and almost immediately produced what in relative terms I shall call 'successful' scenes. At this time I was still a 'lone wolf' modeller in the attic, but I started to photograph my efforts, and had my first articles published, which really encouraged me to think I was getting somewhere.

It's also important that I cover this period first because I very much enjoyed detailing scenery in this scale, as it allows more scope for all kinds of things like allotments, gardens, industrial clutter, building interiors, etc (and there are many more proprietary items available nowadays). I sometimes feel like going back to it, and maybe I will one day. (The trouble is, you can't do everything, even if you want to!)

However, I became aware of how much bigger a slice of countryside would fit into the same physical space in a scale twice as small, so, as this became a more desirable goal, it was inevitable that I should eventually move on to 'N' gauge, the scale in which I have felt at home for the last 12 years or so. But before I move on to that, in my round-the-room attic layout I decided to concentrate on one section at a time, effectively introducing my own 'modular' system, though at the time I hadn't heard of this relatively new concept. I still had a train running right round, but I redesigned and rebuilt the whole thing over time, producing what became four distinct layouts, but all based on the scenery of North Wales. For the first time I photographed and scratchbuilt models of actual houses and other buildings, including 'Bodarfryn', the house on the hill, which was our home for 16 years, and Harlech station and signal box, of which more in a moment.

I also constructed a hillside and tunnel using polystyrene blocks skimmed with Carlite bonding plaster, which is quite light and sets very smoothly so that it doesn't crumble. On the module next to this I built a viaduct over a river, with a mountain background painted by my mother. The tunnel had a lift-off 'lid' for track access, and on it I made a model of 'Clogwyn', the holiday cottage used by generations of our family and friends, a theme I took up in a later 'N' gauge diorama (see Chapter 3). For the water in the river I used resin, which at the time I felt was a really daring venture. It worked quite well, though the smell did not meet with the approval of my wife, and I have not used it since! Nowadays there are quite a number of easy-to-use materials available for making water, though I occasionally still use varnish, which is quite effective if you have prepared the ground carefully. (See Chapter 5 for more on the subject of water.)

So here is a selection of some of these scenes, with a brief description of the materials and methods I used. Bear in mind that this was before the days of so many easily available scenic materials, and also when I had even less to spend than I have today! Also, it was before I got into the sort of panoramic scenery sweep perspective of my smaller-scale models, which is what I'm best known for, and which came later when I turned to 'N' gauge.

'Bodarfryn'

The most striking features of this layout, the first of those that I counted as having reasonably effective scenery, were undoubtedly the hillside with the tunnel underneath, and the adjacent viaduct over the river. Of the original layout, these are the only two sections still in existence, as I couldn't bear to break them up when we decided to retire to a small cottage. They are now owned by Gerry Baker, a fellow enthusiast and co-operator at shows, who may use them as part of a new layout now he's retired.

The hills and terrain levels were made of thick

The viaduct and river on the 'Bodarfryn' layout. The background was painted by my mother.

polystyrene sheet, cut roughly to size and stuck together and on to hardboard with PVA, then shaped with a kitchen knife, finally being skimmed with plaster. The river bed was also formed essentially from plaster brushed to shape, and embedded with sand and gravel while still soft. The ground cover and rocks were then painted, and textured with scatters, sawdust and chippings; the ploughed field is furrowed and painted plaster, while other fields are of lint, and grass-matting. The pine trees were bought, and the deciduous trees and bushes were of textured lichen or wire wool.

The scene was completed with various bought accessories – people, lamps, fencing, wire drums and telegraph poles, but I also scratchbuilt (non-functional) catenary masts from plastic strip and wire, electricity transformers from plastic, poles from drinking straws, and rowing boats of cardboard round balsa-wood formers. The viaduct was hardboard on a wooden frame, covered with brick paper.

The general colouring was a bit garish and blotchy, and of course now I would use only water-based paint and more refined texturing materials.

Part of 'Bodarfryn', showing the tunnel and the end of the viaduct.

Above right 'Clogwyn' cottage on the hillside of the 'Bodarfryn' layout.

Right 'Bodarfryn', the house on the hill.

'Harlech'

However, I was sufficiently encouraged by the results to go on to make another module on the other side of the attic, and this I called 'Harlech', because its main structural features were models of Harlech station and signal box, and also the well-known 'Plas' café on the main street. However, I had recognised the shortcomings of 'Bodarfryn' in regard to the detailing, texturing, and standard of building construction.

Before embarking on the new module, I made a 'test piece' of scenery on a piece of board – a lake with an imaginary castle. On this I tried out bleached carpet underfelt for rough grass, and textured rubberised horsehair for trees and bushes (basic ideas from Barry Norman's *Landscape Modelling*). I also made reeds and flowers from brush bristles.

The buildings were made from a shell of mount board (sometimes known as framing card), faced (if necessary) with brick paper or Slater's Plastikard. The glazing is plastic sheet with Slater's microstrip frames, or Downesglaze windows. As I still use the same basic method today in 'N' gauge, I will deal with the construction in more detail later (see Chapter 4). The estuary features homemade boats, which I also still make in the same way in 'N' gauge (see Chapter 6).

What I consider perhaps the best development, and the chief reason I might one day go back to 'OO' gauge, was my allotments and recreation ground. There are huts and a hen-house of mount board, with plastic rod posts, silver-painted net curtain chicken wire, cloches of left-over bus window-frames, plants of painted wood shavings or strips of scourers and rubberised horsehair, and greenhouses scratchbuilt with plastic sheet, micro-strip frames and Plastikard brick base walls. The tennis court has sugar-paper ground marked out with white microstrip, a fence of silver-painted net curtain, and cocktail-stick posts. The bowling green has a surface of green card with a mount board surround. Although I still do gardens in 'N' gauge, you can only really hint at the detail at a scale of 2mm to the foot!

The 'Harlech' 'test piece': the lake with the imaginary castle.

Above 'Harlech' station on the layout of the same name.

Below The allotments by the station on the 'Harlech' layout.

Above 'Harlech' station building. The roof tiles are 'Superquick' paper and the barge boards are cereal packet card painted with Humbrol enamel. (These days I mainly use acrylics for this kind of work, as it's easier to wash the brushes if you're continually changing colour.) The gutters and downspouts are Dornaplas, Slater's, or just ordinary card. The chimneys are rolled up and glued sugar paper – I also use cocktail stick pieces, plastic drinking straws, etc.

Right 'Plas' Café was then my favourite building, because we used to go and sit on the veranda overlooking the sand-dunes and order a cream scone, which we still occasionally do today! You can see that Downesglaze engine shed windows have many uses!

Left 'Harlech' signal box has chimney cowls of painted cocktail stick pieces with rolled-up paper strips stuck on, and white paper strips for planking. In my 'N' gauge American phase, I used this technique a lot, also with cereal packet card, as you'll see later.

'Dorothea' and 'The Cambrian Connection'

These were the third and fourth modules on my 'OO' gauge attic layout. 'Dorothea' is the name of the local disused quarry in Talysarn, infamous for being a dangerous magnet for adventurous divers, as it is very deep and full of water. I made a model of the old pumphouse surrounded by (probably overscale) bits of slate; note also the factory buildings.

'The Cambrian Connection' was to date my final 'OO' gauge layout. Perhaps the best feature was the harbour, with sea waves of brushed-up plaster painted and varnished. The houses in the fishing village are again (naturally) made from mount board, which by then had become my standard method.

The railway embankment was also, I think, worthy of note, as it crossed quite a realistic-looking stream of varnish, bordered by grass, flowers and vegetation.

A DMU crossing the embankment on 'The Cambrian Connection' layout.

Above The harbour on 'The Cambrian Connection'.

Below The collection of houses that formed the fishing village on 'The Cambrian Connection', together with the harbour, was attributable more to Cornwall than North Wales, it has to be said. (And credit to 'Jamaica Reach' and its creators, one of my all-time favourite layouts; I have since met the members of the North Devon MRC and told them how much they inspired me.)

Right For the factory building on 'Dorothea' I made extensive use of corrugated Plastikard, as well as the cardboard tubes from the centre of aluminium foil rolls. The windows and doors are Peco, if I remember correctly, and the workmen Dapol (but painted by me). Piping, barrels, crates and steps are from the Knightwing range (I don't know if they're still available).

Below A selection of houses in 'OO' scale.

'OO' buildings

Although I didn't photograph the construction stages of the buildings I made for the foregoing modules, and will go into my methods again in the section on 'N' gauge buildings, I still think it is appropriate to describe what I did then.

I started scratchbuilding because I wanted to make a model of 'Bodarfryn', the house we lived in at the time, and also the two holiday cottages where we spent many happy hours while the children were growing up. At first I tried ordinary card, but it did not give a sufficiently solid finish. Then I read an article about mount board, and immediately found it to be suitable. (You can buy it in sheets or as off-cuts from art shops).

You do need a sharp craft knife and a steel ruler, and getting the corners of window-frames square requires a bit of practice and patience. (I still find myself having to re-do bits where I've gone wrong, and sometimes they're still not quite right even then, so don't worry!) Also, it's best to have a self-healing cutting board, which you can get at model shops in various sizes.

For some of the buildings, which here in North Wales are rendered and whitewashed, the basic mount board shell was enough to give the right effect (of course they can be painted or skimmed very lightly with filler or similar). Others need facing with Slater's Plastikard, or other plastic card – brick, stone or whatever is appropriate. I mainly used Downesglaze windows, though one or two have Wills window frames, and if none of these fitted I made my own with plastic sheet and microstrip.

In the left foreground of the lower photograph on the previous page is the shell of the house in the right foreground, giving the basic idea of its construction. Note that I stuck the Plastikard on to each mount board wall separately with Evostik before assembly, because then I could turn it over and cut out the required shape using the mount board as a template, as well as leaving an overlap on every other adjoining wall. (See also Chapter 4 on 'N' gauge construction for more detail.) At the back of the picture are the first versions of 'Clogwyn' and 'Tŷ Mawr', the two holiday cottages, faced with 'Superquick' brick paper, so you can see how the two in front of them were a definite improvement.

A close-up of the 4mm scale model of 'Bodarfryn'.

2
MOVING ON TO 'N' GAUGE

Once having decided that 'N' gauge offered increased possibilities for scenery, and inspired by Richard Coy's well-known 'Porkington' layout, I constructed a model of what I considered to be an archetypal North Wales valley scene, called 'Dyffryn', and in terms of its scenic modelling this became the benchmark for my subsequent efforts.

Unfortunately, however, I did not construct the baseboard of 'Dyffryn' Mark 1 well enough for it to be easily carried or put together, a mistake I have not made since. It only had one line running round, which was not operationally very interesting, and anyway at the time family and fostering commitments still made it impossible for me to contemplate exhibiting. I went on to complete 'Dyffryn' Mark 2 with a double track and sidings – a different scene in many ways, but an attempt to compensate for my earlier lack of foresight (see the photographs overleaf).

It was the geographical landscape aspect of this layout that made me feel I had moved forward in modelling terms, but I had still not developed my own interpretation of 3-D backgrounds, the blending of foreground and background, and working from photographs of prototypes and models, which came with my subsequent series of American layouts.

'Shelby's Landing' and beyond

If I have explained myself well enough, it should by now be clear that I am following a chronological progression in my modelling development in order to throw light on how I model today, so that you can derive the maximum benefit from my experience and avoid making some of my mistakes. (This does not of course preclude my continuing to improve, or make mistakes, as I'm sure that my learning curve is ongoing, as it is for everyone else.)

But I digress! The creation of 'Shelby's Landing' marked the second major turning point in my modelling development, because it was the first time I deliberately constructed a portable layout with a view to exhibiting it. It was also the first time that most, though not all, of my present methods were put to use.

The fact that it is an American outline layout was due to my desire to extend my scenic range, and the USA provides almost endless opportunities for the scenic modeller (as do many other countries, but at the time the available American rolling stock was better and cheaper). With this layout for the first time I employed what I call the 3-D effect (see the photograph on page 27), and attempted for the first time to blend background and foreground, working from photographs of American scenes and structures. I deliberately set out to get the overall effect that I now strive after in every scene I make.

The 3-D background effect

Up to this point I had only used two-dimensional ready-printed backscenes or roughly painted hardboard for a background, but now that I was trying to create a more refined, much smaller-scale American cameo, I needed to improve in this department.

Even now, after ten years and six American layouts, I've never visited the USA, but of course I have been reading articles (on both model and prototype) in American magazines (and *Continental Modeller*) for the last 13 years or more.

Above The single-track 'Dyffryn' Mark 1.

Below 'Dyffryn' Mark 2, now with double track.

The quayside on 'Shelby's Landing'. Note the photographic backscene, adding depth.

Left Materials required to create a 3-D backscene.

Below I assembled a series of three pictures – distant mountains, a wooded hillside and a lake – overlapped them a little and stuck them lightly together so that the top edges were still slightly raised, giving an impression of depth.

Below The finished scene. I modelled the hills in front to fit, and dabbed on a wash of blue stippled with white for the sky. Then I added the stream as if disappearing into the lake.

Above Cut-out buildings and trees – you can also use the same basic idea with buildings, and with ready-made background sheets.

Below Note the effective '3-D' background on the 'Cobra Canyon' layout.

From these I have built up a collection of photos, and right at the beginning I cut out suitable pictures of scenery, some of which I used in a small background section on 'Shelby's Landing'. The accompanying photographs demonstrate the technique. (On subsequent layouts, I also stuck each picture onto card, which reinforced the effect – see photographs of 'Rocky Ridge' and 'Cobra Canyon'.)

It's also important to bear in mind how to make the background and foreground blend so that the distance effect is enhanced. I try to achieve this by using finer, lighter scatters and colours on the hills or fields at the back, gradually increasing and darkening items as they come forward, maybe with a fence or hedge in between. I am not an artist – I am just trying to reproduce the kind of effect I see in photos.

Constructing the baseboard

Although this book is about scenery, and there are lots of books and magazine articles that cover the topic of baseboard construction, many to a high degree of detail and professionalism (and some requiring tools and skills that I don't have), I nonetheless think it appropriate here to describe the way I now make all my baseboards, having settled on a practical and easily repeatable format. Of course, in my case the reason is that I want to be able to do this as quickly as possible so I can proceed to making the scenery. However, in each case I have to consider beforehand the particular requirements of the scene I am making, as that partly dictates the shapes and levels of the ground and trackbed.

The first four of my portable 'N' gauge layouts were slightly different from what I do now, as they weren't 'boxed in'. They were oval-shaped with a hardboard surround and a low hardboard backdrop or scenic divider. The disadvantages of this were that they could not be stacked for storage or transport and, perhaps more importantly, they didn't have the deep and enclosed aspect, which, when my detachable pelmet is added across the front, gives the impression of a complete scene. At one show I attended with 'Die alte Mühle' (before I added the acrylic screens I now mainly use for protection of delicate detailing), a young boy put his head inside the front and said, 'I would like to live in here', which to me was the greatest compliment I could wish for.

From 'Rocky Ridge' onwards the baseboards are all 5 feet by 2ft 6in, and (except for 'Rocky Ridge') 14 inches high, so I can stack two in my car, one on top of the other, using a removable lid made of thin wooden slats to cover the lower one. (I usually take two to an exhibition, as this provides more interest and variety to the viewing public, and makes it more cost effective for the exhibition manager!)

As an example, therefore, I will take my most recent layout, 'Porth Kernow', and show you pictures of its construction from start to finish.

Above right First of all I made an oblong wooden frame of 2 inch by 1 inch softwood. For a whole layout I need about 20 yards of this, to allow a bit extra for knots, odd bits left over or mistakes in cutting, and I usually obtain it from a local builders' merchant, together with a piece of hardboard 8 feet by 4 feet, cut at 5 feet. I screwed and glued the frame pieces together at the corners (without cutting joints, as I don't have a workbench), and countersunk the screw heads so that the hardboard surrounds could be fixed flush later. This oblong was then strengthened by adding crosspieces, specially positioned on this layout to accommodate the lower ground. To this frame I then added four vertical double corner pieces, the outside ones shorter at the front because above them would later be the hole for the pelmet to slot in where the hardboard corners met. Extra crosspieces were laid flat to support the two hardboard surfaces, which would thus be at a lower level to form the base for the river bed and estuary.

Right I then cut out the pieces of hardboard for the sides and front, and tacked and glued them to the base and uprights. The back was fixed only to the upper part of the uprights and, being only 7 inches deep, was strengthened with a length of 2 inch by 1 inch timber, leaving a substantial gap for the trains to run behind and under the hillside later. In the accompanying photograph you can see that I added two extra uprights at the front to complete the walls of the holes into which the pelmet legs would slot. Also, I cut out two access holes in the sides to allow access to the track under the hill. (The one on the right later proved unnecessary and was filled in – my layouts evolve and the plans are always subject to modification!)

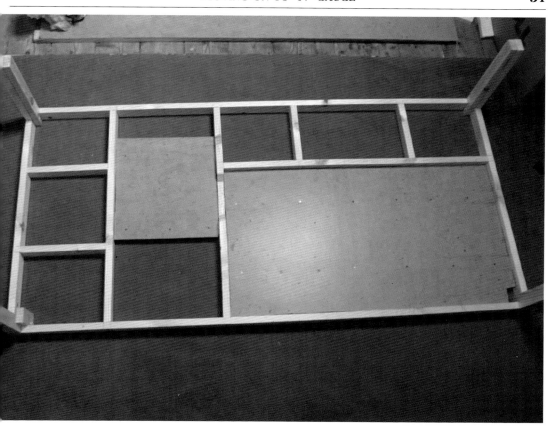

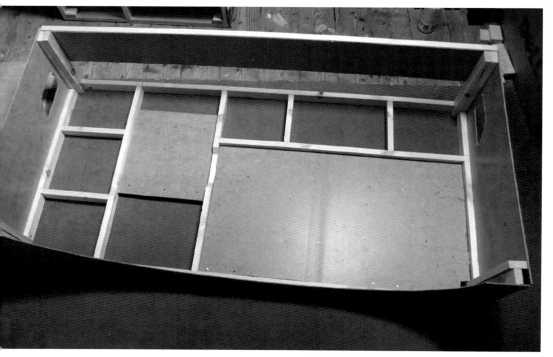

Because in this layout the track level was above ground level, I fixed an elongated 'U' shape of 2 inch by 1 inch timber to blocks of wood fixed to the frame, which stuck out 4 inches at the back. I also added risers round the edge and in the middle where necessary, as seen in the photographs.

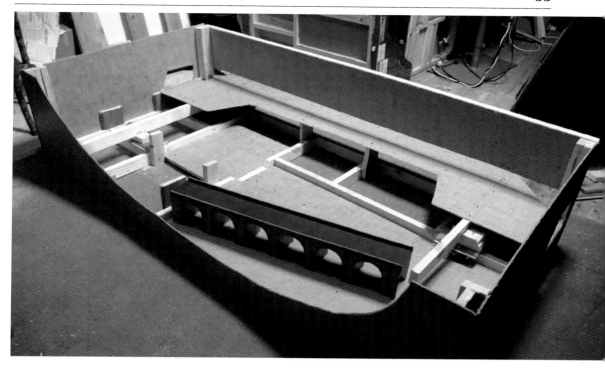

I then cut out a piece of hardboard for the rear of the layout and tacked and glued it in position. The photograph also shows where I sawed and chiselled out a section of the crosspiece to make it level with the hardboard for the river bed. At this point I also positioned the viaduct (which I had already scratchbuilt from hardboard, mount board, card and brick card), ready to align it with the front sections of the hardboard trackbed.

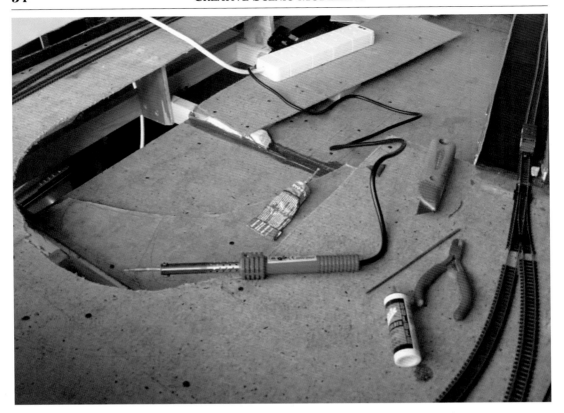

Once all this was done, the next thing was laying the track. For this I used Peco Flextrack, some Setrack curves, and Peco medium-radius Insulfrog points. First I established where the points were going to be – in this case only one was on the scenic section, with the other four at the back providing a passing loop for each of the two lines. So, starting from the set of points at the front I cut and joined up sections with connectors (removing sleepers where necessary, to be replaced later), tested that the guard's van ran over it smoothly, then soldered the outer edges for extra holding and current flow). I stuck down the track with Evostik as I went along, but note that I had already cut a hole in the hardboard to accommodate the point motor rod from beneath, and stuck in place, wired up and tested the point motor. I then drilled holes in the hardboard to feed two wires up to the tracks at each end of each passing loop, soldered them and connected them to my control panel, so I could test-run an engine (the extra feed aids smooth running).

Above right Once the track was stuck down I ballasted it with Woodland Scenics fine grey ballast. I spooned it on, spread it and positioned it with a dry brush, sprayed it with water to make it damp, then syringed onto it a 50/50 mix of water and wood glue. (The Deluxe Materials container was an old one just used here for mixing – the contents were on my 'Caer Faban' layout!) Once set, any gaps were filled in and stuck down, then I cleaned the track and removed excess ballast with a craft knife.

Right All is now complete, with the background sky paper added to the back and sides (left over from a previous background set). In this case there wasn't really enough room for countryside). Note that the rear corners are curved – I added rounded mount board in front of the wooden uprights. I use frame sealant to stick this, as well as the edges of the hardboard at the front corners, and anything else that it's suitable for.

'Caer Faban', one of my layouts built using the method just described, is seen here at the Corris Railway Society's exhibition in 2006. You can see how the pelmet slots into the base to form a frontispiece. That's me next to it, with our youngest daughter Bridget. I don't think I need to say which is which!

3
CREATING A SCENE

Some of the pictures you have already seen (and those that come later, as you've probably had a sneak peek!) will have given you a good idea of the sort of scenes I create, and I hope they were what made you decide to buy the book. (If you're still browsing, don't hesitate any longer – buy it now!)

Planning

At the risk of stating the obvious, I get my inspiration from stretches of scenery and certain buildings, either seen when I'm out and about, or come across in books and magazines. My basic problem is that I want to model just about every evocative scene I see! Initially I limited myself to two main areas – Snowdonia and the American West – but in the last few years I've extended this to North Germany and Cornwall, the first two of which happily have plenty of scope for mountains and valleys or canyons, and the last two also for sea and water features. Of course, you may well want to make a model of something completely different, and so you should, but in my experience it's best to work from photographs that you've collected from various sources, or ones you've taken yourself. However, though some people do it, and with good results, I myself would not set out to re-create an actual prototype location. Even in 2mm scale this requires considerable selective compression, unless you have a lot of space, and it limits creative imagination more than I would find tolerable. Personally I have found it more effective to take the essence of two or three scenes, and blend them into a composite whole that conjures up the atmosphere of a location or area, without restricting my freedom to have variety within the given scene. So 'Dyffryn', for example, is based on

the upper section of the Conwy Valley line around Dolwyddelan and Roman Bridge, but not an exact location, so I have been able to include the station at Roman Bridge as well as the ruined castle at Dolwyddelan – even though they are at least half a mile apart! – and also some houses based on actual prototypes in the area, from Dolwyddelan and Beddgelert.

Basic terrain: from baseboard to hard shell

In one respect the layouts I have built since 'Shelby's Landing' are different, and I hope better for it – they have more depth, and consequently needed larger amounts of scenic contouring, for which I started using the card lattice technique I still employ. You can of course use polystyrene, which I do use here and there, but as I usually utilise the space under hillsides for passing loops, I find the card lattice method more practical, even if it is a bit more time-consuming.

Having finally arrived at, in a sense, the starting point of my current practice in making scenery, I now propose to devote the next chapters to a more detailed look at my modelling methods.

As you saw in the photographs on pages 8-9, the basis for all my scenery is the hard shell, which covers all except the trackbed and level ground – of which there is not usually very much on my layouts! (The two German layouts are the exception to this, being set in the flat lowland of Schleswig Holstein.)

In the last chapter I used 'Porth Kernow' as an example of how I usually construct a baseboard for a layout, so now I will continue to use it to show you how I make the hard shell for the scenery. As you saw in the photograph on page 35, the

Above Roman Bridge station on the 'Dyffryn' layout.

Below The baseboard, tunnel entrances and mount board screening on 'Porth Kernow'.

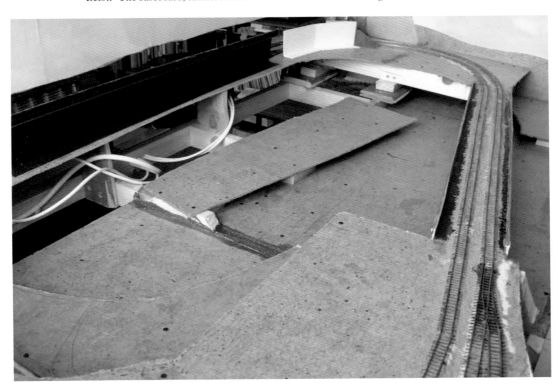

baseboard was now ready for this, and had been constructed with three levels for river, lower ground, and track on higher ground, complete with ballasted track and scenic surround. Of course it is not absolutely necessary to have the trackwork complete at this stage, but I like to feel that the working part is finished before I get on to the scenery proper – and you certainly need to have the trackbed done and know where the track is going before you make the scenery contours.

Now for the exciting part of scenic modelling, when you can really start to feel that your diorama is beginning to take shape! However, even here a little preparation is necessary before the hard shell itself can be formed. I first positioned and stuck the two tunnel entrances, and cut and glued lengths of mount board to them and along the front of the passing loops on the rear trackbed. This was to ensure access to the track once the hillside was made, and also to support the card lattice as it was constructed across it.

I then cut strips of cereal packet card and stapled them together to make a lattice, the ends of which I stuck along the scenery background and along the ground level. I put the unmarked side up, not so that anyone looking later at my 'fiddle yard' round the back could see that I eat Weetabix for breakfast – it was just to make sure that none of the printing was visible through the sheet! This process was repeated for other parts of the baseboard where hills were required.

Once this was all finished, I cut pieces of old sheet to cover the lattice. I then mixed a small amount of water and PVA glue in a bowl and soaked the pieces of sheet in it before draping them over the lattice. At this stage you can still see the lattice underneath, but I knew it would disappear later.

I used to use filler for making the hard shell, and of course there are proprietary brands of material that can be soaked and draped over whatever framework you've made – for example, 'Modroc' – but I find my method easy, cheap and, above all, light, which at my time of life is an important consideration.

I will now move on to painting and texturing more generally, but still using some illustrations from 'Porth Kernow' where appropriate.

The card lattice with pieces of sheet laid over it.

Above The PVA and water mix.

Below The PVA-impregnated sheet in place.

Painting

Of course, you could paint all the ground cover at this stage, but there's not much point until you know at least roughly where you are going to have rocks, fields, roads, buildings, etc; and in any case your rough ground may well be quite varied. However, how you go from here depends on a bit of forward planning.

By this stage of constructing a layout, I have usually already made a collection of buildings or structures appropriate to the prototype, and have a rough idea where they might go. I've always got an initial plan, which includes reference to a village, mine, harbour, bridge or whatever, but find it difficult to imagine my final version of a three-dimensional scene on a two-dimensional plan. So quite often, when I'm ready to position my structures on the layout, I decide to make modifications or even quite significant changes to my original plan.

I now mark out in pencil the areas that are definitely going to be covered by specific items, and do an initial paint covering on the rest. (In some cases, a building or structure has already been set into the ground cover, for example the ruined castle on 'Dyffryn', or the gravel loaders on 'North West Valley Lines').

To start with, it's mainly a matter of applying a coating of an approximate shade, and erring on the lighter side, because it's easier to darken than lighten later. Thus rough grass areas would obviously be light green, and earth a brownish colour. (I keep trying to match the shade to the photos I'm working from.) Most, though not necessarily all, is going to be textured anyway, and you can always do a final touching up (I sometimes keep a mix of a particular shade in a separate pot specially).

As to what kind of paint, as I have already mentioned I almost only use the water-based variety, mainly 'testers' or 'match pots' from DIY stores, because they are quite economical, a handy size, and most important of all come in a range of shades that include what I call 'earth colours' – often difficult to describe, and with exotic-sounding names, but which lend themselves to mixing and matching. Different firms have different ranges, and they also vary over time, so it's best to choose them according to the colour rather than the name. To give you some idea, examples I have used include Peppercorn, Biscuit, Dijon

The painted hard shell.

Delight, Oatmeal, Nectarine, Pomegranate, Morning Primrose, Yellow Ochre, Wild Moss, Raw Umber, Gold Leaf, Taupe, Sunflower and Honey, as well as basic greens and browns.

In addition, I have a selection of small pots or tubes of acrylic paints, including bright basic colours, which as well as occasionally being added to ground cover mixes, are also used for structures and boats, etc. On buildings I also use emulsion paints. I also keep a pot of black powder paint, so I can darken a mixture if necessary without changing the basic shade.

On 'Porth Kernow' I painted all the hard shell, except where I put rocks, with one colour, Forest Walk by name, because I liked it, and knew that all the surface would be fields, trees, hedges and bushes. I usually add the rocks first to establish their position, but for more on this subject see Chapter 5.

Texturing

This is a big subject area, and could take a whole chapter, but I don't want to risk boring you! I'll just outline some of my basic procedures, then mention specific details when I deal with particular scenes later on.

There are so many products on the market, with new ones being added all the time, that I can't claim knowledge or experience of everything that's available, so confining myself mainly to those that I use doesn't mean there aren't others that would do just as well. In any case, with this as with other areas of modelling, there are a variety of ways of using materials – showing you how I operate doesn't mean that you shouldn't experiment with alternatives of your own. And of course I select the materials I use for my kind of scene and scale, which in your case might be quite different.

For general texturing I used to use mainly Woodland Scenics turf – fine, coarse and extra coarse, light and dark green, yellow grass and burnt grass, earth blend, foliage and talus, augmented by real sand and gravel. Latterly, however, I have also been using lots of Auhagen, Busch, Heki and Noch foliage grass and other materials, as well as a range of other products

Texturing on the 'Porth Kernow' layout.

A general view of 'Dyffryn' showing the texturing effects.

made by different firms, as and when I see something I like the look of.

For hedges I use as a base polyfibre, kitchen scourer, rubberised horsehair or even loofah, while for rough grass I use things like old towelling dyed green, scatters or fine foliage materials, Woodland Scenics field grass or similar. For grazed fields I use dyed lint and occasionally the better-quality grass matting.

Remember that what I'm describing here is in 2mm scale, which means that everything is very small, and in terms of general ground cover you're often just hinting at things rather than making detailed replicas. In 'OO'/4mm scale there would inevitably be more detailing involved.

I'll describe some more detailed texturing later when I come to gardens, etc, but here I'm looking at what is really the areas between fields,

rocks, trees, etc. Take my 'Dyffryn' layout, for example. To texture the rough ground here, I first of all brushed on slightly diluted PVA, covering one section at a time. Then I positioned bits of Woodland Scenics clump foliage to represent gorse bushes, then areas of Woodland Scenics coarse turf to represent rough grass, followed by smaller amounts of fine turf, then some sand. Note that I work from larger to smaller materials, as they blend in better and look more natural that way. When this had dried, I vacuumed up the loose excess, then brushed on PVA in certain selected patches to add scatter or foliage to represent flowers or weeds, repeating the process if necessary till I thought it looked right. Finally, I dabbed acrylic bright yellow on to the clump foliage to represent the gorse flowers.

4
SCRATCHBUILDING STRUCTURES

Once I've decided on a setting for a layout, and drawn up an initial plan, I collect pictures of the sort of buildings I might feature on it, particularly the houses. I like to have a few structures finished in some cases even before I've started building the baseboard, because their construction is really the most fundamental as well as time-consuming element in the whole process.

It's also possible to make them while sitting comfortably at my front-room table during the winter months, instead of scrabbling around in the cold attic! In fact, I now make some sections of scenery incorporating buildings on separate pieces of hardboard and introduce these sections to the layout baseboard at a later stage. Then, when I'm in the final stages of detailing the main layout, I have it all on my table during modelling sessions, just storing it vertically behind the door in the interim (not possible when family or friends are staying!). Apart from meeting friendly and interesting people at shows, I'm never happier than sitting at my table creating these more detailed items.

The accompanying pictures show my basic scratchbuilding technique, and although these are in 2mm scale, it is essentially the same method as I used for 4mm.

The house at Beddgelert

This model is a key building on my second 'Dyffryn' layout, having been saved from the first version.

Below left Working from a photograph, I cut out the shape of the front wall in mount board. I don't measure everything exactly, but in 2mm scale a person is about 11mm tall (and I have the Downesglaze windows as a guide). In this case I also needed a porch, for which I used cereal packet card. I marked and cut out the window and door frames, having marked them out using the glazing and porch pieces. Then I painted the porch, door and window frames the appropriate colour, using a small acrylic pot. For doors I use pieces of cereal packet card cut to size and painted the appropriate colour. If, as usual (and easiest!), the door is shut, I leave an overlap all round, and simply stick the card on the inside of the frame when dry; sometimes I draw panels on the door with a black biro, and occasionally put in glazing, though in 'N' gauge this is very small and therefore fiddly.

Right Note at the side of my cutting board my basic tools and materials: glue, scissors, craft knife, acrylic paint pots and paint brush, and a photograph of a curtain pattern cut from a glossy magazine. I cut out the sides and back of the house from mount board, and likewise the window and door frames. (In this instance, I'm leaving the back and one side wall blank, as they won't be visible on the model.) If the model is to be faced with Plastikard, in this case stone, I lie the Plastikard face down and stick onto it a sheet of card using Evostik. I then turn it over and cut out the shape, using the mount board as a guide, but leaving the width of the Plastikard as excess on the front and back walls, so that the side walls will fit snugly into them on assembly. Before doing that, though, I stick in the window glazing, and add curtains if necessary.

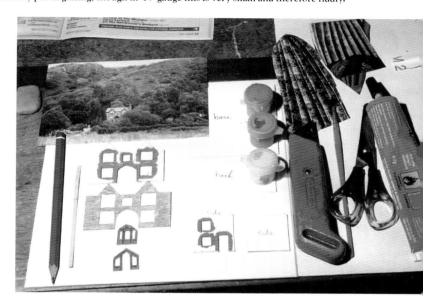

Below Having assembled the walls, I then cut roof pieces from mount board to fit. I make a length of chimney stack out of cereal packet card, faced with the same stone Plastikard as used for the walls, and cut out a hole in the roof pieces before assembly to accommodate it. The stonework is painted an appropriate stone colour. Sometimes I first brush white over the Plastikard, then wipe off the excess to highlight the mortar joints.

Left I position and fix the chimney, and face the roof with tile Plastikard, also cutting out and sticking two little triangles of Plastikard for the roof sections over the bedroom windows. The barge boards are made from cereal packet card, the gutter is plastic strip and the downspout plastic rod.

Below left The house is then stuck on to a piece of mount board, a garden marked out, and the path painted. The lawns are made of little pieces of grass mat, and the flower beds are painted earth colour, then brushed with PVA, on to which bits of foliage material and scatter are carefully dropped, to be painted appropriate bright colours when dry. Strips of kitchen scourer dipped in scatter form the hedges, while foliage clumps or polyfibre dipped in scatter make the hedges.

Above The house and garden are completed with a tree, greenhouse and people (all bought items in this instance). The row of houses on the left are based on those next to the pub in Dolwyddelan.

Right Another house, whose prototype is in Barmouth, made in the same way.

'Clogwyn'

I made this model of the holiday cottage in 2mm scale for my layout of the same name.

Below Four stages in the construction of 'Clogwyn' cottage. First come photographs of the prototype. The second stage shows how I cut strips of green paper (from a glossy magazine) to make the window frames for the front and rear windows. In the case of the front windows I stuck them over the white

Downesglaze frames (although it's a bit difficult to see as they're on the green cutting board). Stage three was cutting out the walls from mount board with their window openings, and stage four the addition of the stone Plastikard, behind which the door and windows were then stuck in place. I added a woodshed made in the same way, then the roof and chimneys, the stacks being made from fine sandpaper on a card shell, with Blu-tack and cocktail stick cowlings, all painted in shades of grey. The stone was painted with different shades of acrylic khaki to pick out individual stones, after highlighting the mortar with cream.

Below left I marked out and roughly painted the garden on a piece of mount board, then cut and shaped stone slabs of cereal packet card, with which I built up the garden walls, painting them the same colour as the cottage walls.

Above Finally the garden was textured with coarse grass material, lichen, foliage and scatter.

Below The completed model on the 'Clogwyn' layout.

Other buildings

The shell of all the buildings I construct is made in the same basic way I have just described. Likewise, for stations, huts and small office-type structures there is really no need for me to elaborate further; by looking at them in the photographs of the cameo scenes and general views of layouts it should be obvious whether they are faced with Plastikard or similar, in brick, stone, planking, tiling, etc.

For larger buildings such as a mine, logging complex, gravel loader and stone crusher, which all feature on the American layouts, I made extensive use of matchwood, as well as thin strips of cereal packet card and paper. (You can buy matchwood for modelling in bags of 1,000 for £2-£3 – I'm still using the only one I ever bought, and still have plenty left!)

Again, it should be possible to identify the materials by looking at the pictures. On 'Shelby's Landing', for example, the main logging shed walls are faced with strips of card, as is the roof of the small depot above the top line, while the roof is lined with thin strips of ordinary white paper. The grey finish in this case is a mixture of white emulsion and black powder paint.

Exactly the same methods and materials are used for the gravel loader and huts on several layouts, sometimes with the addition of matchwood on the front face of the main building as well as for the supporting structure. This feature is particularly prominent on the gravel loaders in the harbour of 'High Peaks Railroad' and on the right-hand loader of 'North West Valley Lines'. On the other hand, for the mine buildings on 'High Peaks Railroad' and 'Rocky Ridge' I made extensive use of plastic card, principally Slater's Plastikard, although other makes are available.

The logging pond and sheds on 'Shelby's Landing'.

The mine and gravel loader on 'High Peaks Railroad'.

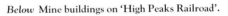

Above The right-hand-side gravel loader on 'North West Valley Lines'.

Below Mine buildings on 'High Peaks Railroad'.

The mine building on the 'Rocky Ridge' layout.

Trestle bridges

Finally in this chapter we take a look at some other structures, giving a more detailed account of how they were made; although these are also based on American prototypes, the same techniques and materials could be used for British or Continental versions, and indeed for any other remotely similar structures worldwide.

Trestle bridges are mainly found in the USA, but not exclusively, and they are a good example of the sort of structure you can build with a template, as shown in the photographs.

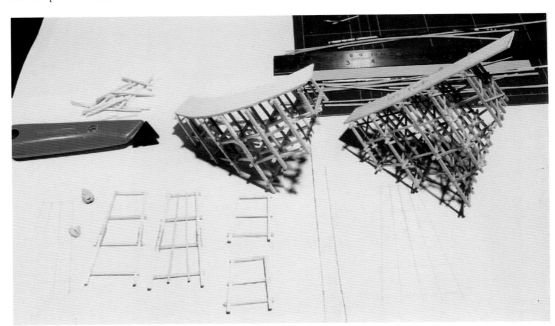

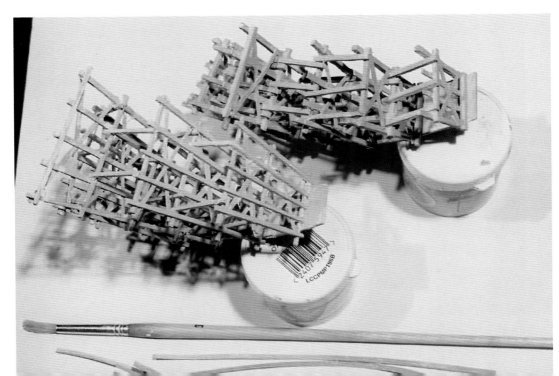

Below left These two templates were used for the two trestle bridges I built for my 'Pelican Creek' layout. (In the end I built three for it, and subsequently lots more for other layouts – positive comments at shows indicate that they are a feature well worth including, and quite easy to do.) The cross-struts were added and stuck with PVA, the legs being held to the card with Blu-Tack. Then the length of the legs was adjusted to fit the place in the canyon where they were to be positioned, and each section was then stuck upside-down and evenly spaced on a mount board shaped to correspond to the curve of the track bed.

Bottom left Next more cross-struts were added at right-angles between the so far two-dimensional leg structures, and the whole thing was painted grey.

Above The main trestle bridge on 'Cobra Canyon'.

Right Trestle bridges on the left-hand side of 'Rocky Ridge'.

A general view of 'North West Valley Lines' showing a variety of trestle bridges.

Tunnel entrances

With their retaining walls, these again feature mainly on my American layouts; for British-outline layouts I have quite often used Peco tunnel mouths, as they look quite authentic and can't really be improved upon.

Right The tunnel entrance and side walls are cut from a sheet of mount board. The entrance is faced with thinner card round the edges and scribed to represent a brick, stone or wood arch, then both it and the wall pieces are edged and sectioned with matchwood, then painted.

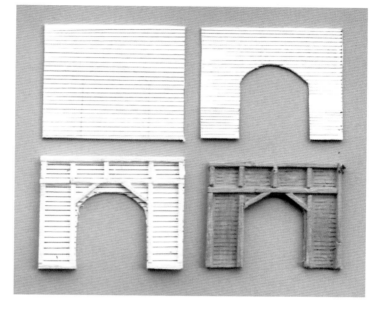

Below Tunnel mouths on 'Rocky Ridge'.

Tunnel mouths abound on the 'Cobra Canyon' layout.

5
NATURAL FEATURES

In this chapter I will look at more specific natural elements of scenery that I didn't cover in Chapter 4, such as fields, rocks, water, trees and flowers. Of course this list is not exhaustive and, as I mentioned before, there are different ways of making all these things. I am not attempting to give you a complete overview of the subject, although I will mention some alternative methods and materials as appropriate.

Water

I'm not saying that I'm very old, but I'm getting on in years, and even in the last 15 years, since I've been seriously into scenic modelling, the range of materials available for making water has increased beyond all recognition, so it's hard for someone like me to keep track of them all, and more particularly, to try out different ones each time I build a new layout, which is usually every year! (All my layouts have a water feature, as I'm convinced it always enhances a scene, and is usually very effective, even if in small quantities.)

Let me therefore comment on the three proprietary examples I have used most on recent layouts, and mention some of the others I have used in the past.

Deluxe Materials 'Scenic Water' was used for the estuaries on 'Clogwyn' and 'Caer Faban', and also the culvert streams on 'Cobra Canyon'. You may have used it yourself; it comes in a tub, which you merely sit in a bowl of hot water till it melts, then pour it on – very easy, and quite effective. You have to be careful that the edges don't set rounded if you are not just filling in a pond or a harbour, as it does set quickly. However, that can be an advantage if you are making a mountain stream, for example, because you can just dribble it on and

let it run into position, though it may need a bit of persuasion!

Javis 'Countryside Water' was used for the rivers on 'Cobra Canyon', 'Die alte Mühle' and 'Porth Kernow'. This is a viscous liquid you buy in a plastic bottle, and you simply pour it on slowly, though only to a depth of a few millimetres. In marked contrast to the 'Scenic Water', it takes up to two and a half days to set, but when it finally starts to harden you can brush it or scrape it into ripples. (If they smooth out, just repeat till they stay put!) In my experience, it produces the most realistic results, though it requires patience.

Busch 'Aqua' was used on 'Der Nordseehafen', and comes in a plastic bottle. It is not too runny; when you squeeze it on it more or less spreads itself, though it may need a little help. (I used a glue spreader.) To start with it is white, but as it sets this goes, and it ripples itself. Like 'Countryside Water', it must not be applied too thickly or it won't easily set.

I have also used Woodland Scenics 'E-Z Water' (on 'Pelican Creek' and the stream on 'North West Valley Lines'). It is very like 'Countryside Water' and produces similar results, except that it is in globules and sets quickly.

I only used boat resin once, for the river on 'Bodarfryn'; it was very pungent and slow, but effective in the end. Once or twice I have used colourless bath sealant (notably the river and waterfall on 'Dyffryn'), but this was before the latest products became available, and was, I think, less effective. (I know there are now new materials for rushing water and waterfalls, but I haven't tried them as yet.) A number of times I tried varnish, on 'Shelby's Landing' and 'North West

Two views of the river and harbour on 'Porth Kernow', for which I used Javis's 'Countryside Water'.

For the harbour on 'North West Valley Lines' I used Woodland Scenics 'E-Z Water'.

The water in the harbour on 'Der Nordseehafen' is Busch 'Aqua'.

Valley Lines', for example; it is quite effective, but may need several layers, and will try to escape given half a chance. Don't leave it over the best Axminster without a safety net!

It may be stating the obvious, but the effectiveness of your 'water' does depend to a great extent on what it is poured on to. When people ask me what the water is made of, they may not realise that, while applying it took only minutes, getting the river or lake bed ready to receive it took lots of sessions of applying sand and gravel, scatters, grass tufts and foliage clumps, etc, till I felt it looked right.

I cannot emphasise enough that, in this as in other aspects of scenic modelling (in my experience at least!), a lot of the time it is trial and error and expenditure of time and patience. Getting the whole scene to 'gel' involves constant

reference to the photograph(s) of the scene you are trying to re-create, endeavouring to translate 'reality' into what is believable in model terms. This often means highlighting certain features and leaving out others, till you get to the most convincing 3-D 'picture' within your scope, which may be quite removed from your starting point!

While on the subject of water I think it is appropriate to mention that for making mud, as in harbours or estuaries, I now always use brown frame sealant, which comes in a tube, is cheap, and can easily be squirted on, spread out and brushed, using some water, so it sets in little pools and channels like the real thing. Also its flat surfaces can be painted a lighter sandier brown after it has dried, leaving the channels darker to increase its effect.

Rocks

In the past I used to make rocks with plaster or filler, sometimes shaping it myself and sometimes using Woodland Scenics rubber moulds. However, over the last few years my preferred method of making rocks is with 'Sculptamold', an American product that comes in plastic bags; these are about 3lb and cost no more than £6 as I write, obtainable in Britain from one or two of the big model shops, and some smaller ones if you ask around. The question I'm most frequently asked at shows is how I make my rocks, and I'm sure that a good part of the reason is that with 'Sculptamold' it's quite easy to get good results. (I have to declare at this point that I have no connection with the firm that makes it, and no commercial link to any of its outlets!)

First of all, as always you need at least one, preferably several, pictures of the sort of rocks you want to model. When I'm modelling rocks for North Wales scenery I take my own photographs, but you can get plenty of any location from books, magazines, or online. Second, I'm assuming that you've already got your hard shell finished, and you know where you actually want your rocks to be.

As in the section on constructing the baseboard, I will use 'Porth Kernow' as an example of how I make rocks, not because they are necessarily the best I have made, but they are fairly typical and I have a sequence of pictures to illustrate the process, which I'm sure gives a better idea than merely describing the end result.

I have put some of the dry powder from the bag into an old plastic container and added water from the jug a little at a time, stirring with the fork till it's nicely wet but not runny, otherwise it won't set. It's best not do too much at once – just enough to put a dollop on your chosen spot. It will even stick to a more or less vertical surface.

Next shape it with a craft knife, screwdriver or small scraper – anything that enables you to get the sharp edges and contours you need. It dries slowly, but if you're still not happy with your efforts after 10 or 15 minutes, you may need to squirt on a little water to keep it malleable for a bit longer (I use an old bathroom spray bottle).

Continue the process, using photos as a guide.

Carry on till most of the rocks are in place. Once you've reached an artistic conclusion, leave it to harden for up to 24 hours, then it's ready for painting.

Right and below When you've mixed a suitable shade with water-based paint, dab some on near the top and spray it, so the colour runs down in rivulets, accentuating the natural contours of the rock, and leaving darker and lighter patches. Dab any areas not covered, spraying again.

Bottom When the paint is dry, repeat the process with a small amount of black paint or India ink, to highlight the cracks and crevices. Some of the paint is absorbed, so even at this stage it may be necessary to add more colour, so I keep a pot of the mixed paint for weeks after.

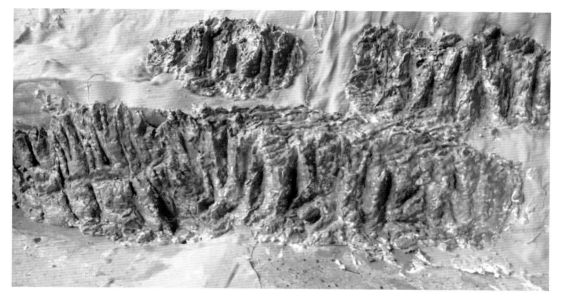

Above Rocks on, appropriately, 'Rocky Ridge'.

Below Rocks on the 'Dyffryn' layout.

Above A Class 25 diesel crosses the viaduct on 'Porth Kernow'. Various styles of grass can be seen.

Below Fields and rough grass on the 'Caer Faban' layout.

More varied styles of grass and foliage seen on the right-hand side of the 'Die alte Mühle' layout.

Flowers

Making flowers in 2mm scale is often little more than setting scatter of the appropriate colour into a border, though the larger varieties can be represented by foliage clumps, lichen or bits of teased-up scourer or similar rough-textured material with coloured scatter or dabs of paint for flowers. In 4mm scale there is more scope, and I often used brush bristles. I keep a brush head in my modelling drawer, and when I need some flowers I brush PVA lightly on a patch of bristles, dip the brush upside down in some scatter material, and leave it to dry.

If you have a can of 'Spraymount' this is even easier, but more expensive – you don't have to wait as long, but the scatter may not set quite so hard. A cheaper alternative is hair spray, though I've never used it, but recently I bought a can of Bostik's 'Fast-Tak', which is reasonably priced and useful for fixing all kinds of foliage and texturing materials.

I then paint the flowers using bright acrylics or even fluorescent paint, then cut and 'plant' them as and where required, setting them in PVA or Evostik. One example is the 'red hot pokers' on the embankment in the photograph on page 21.

6
FINISHING TOUCHES

In this section I'll describe how I scratchbuilt one or two small objects. Most of them are available as proprietary items, but if you like a challenge, and want to be original, the list of possibilities is almost endless. However, even I would not attempt to make things like telegraph poles, telephone kiosks, lamps and most items of lineside furniture in 2mm scale (though I have made some in 4mm in the past!), but it is amazing what you can create with bits of card, paper and plastic, even in 2mm.

Below **Making stone walls.**

Stone walls

To make these I use cereal packet card. I cut it into strips, then cut it again into small pieces with rounded edges, leaving some strips for the base of each section of walling. This process takes ages, and is usually accompanied by either music or a TV programme and liquid refreshment (tea, of course!). The pieces are then stuck down with PVA a layer at a time, starting with the uncut strip for the base. I usually pick up the pieces with the point of my craft knife to position them; tweezers soon get coated in PVA and everything sticks to them!

As each layer takes a while to set, I have several walls (including ruined barns) on the go at the same time.

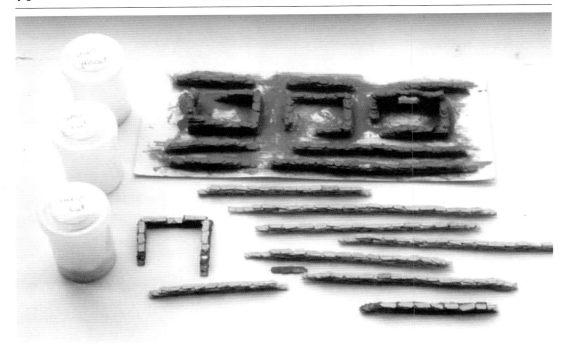

Above Completed stone walls.

Below A stone wall on the 'Clogwyn' layout.

Culvert pipes

This is a relatively easy one for starters, either in 2mm or 4mm, and quite effective, as they stand out in a scene, and are a convenient way of introducing a water feature where there is otherwise no apparent source!

Right I've assembled the sort of materials needed for 2mm scale culvert pipes: dowel wrapped round with Plastikard corrugations, painted grey, and set in card faced with brick Plastikard, topped with a Plastruct angle girder. Alternatively, use a drinking straw and rust-painted thin card. This gives the basic pipe with a brick or concrete surround.

Below A culvert pipe on an American scene I made years ago but did not keep; I don't think something similar would be out of place on a British layout.

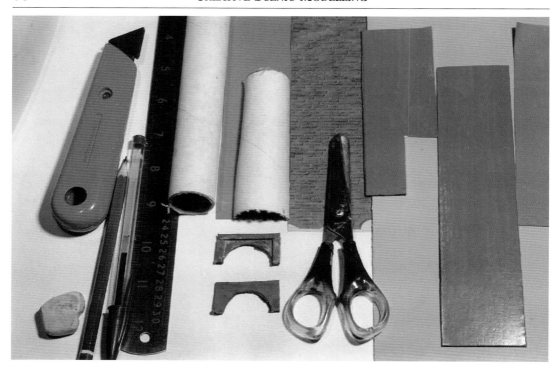

Above The other type of culvert, which I've made in 4mm scale, is like a small bridge. I used the cardboard centre from a kitchen roll cut in half, and pieces of card faced with brick paper or Plastikard.

Below The finished item on the embankment section of my 'Cambrian Connection' layout. When this photograph was taken the track had not been ballasted.

Scratchbuilt road signs

I made these in 2mm scale, together with signal lights, road markings and crossing barriers, specially for my depiction of the level crossing at Harlech, partly because all were not available, and partly as a challenge!

To make 2mm scale road signs I punched holes in thin plastic card painted red and cut out triangles with sides 7mm long from the same card. I then cut smaller circles and triangles from white paper, and stuck them on the red ones.

The backs of the circles and triangles are painted grey, as are lengths of plastic rod, which are then stuck on to form the poles. In the top right-hand corner is an enlarged view of the assembly stage. An oblong sign adds to the range, and a fine black marker pen is used for inscribing the signs. Tweezers and mini crocodile clips come in handy!

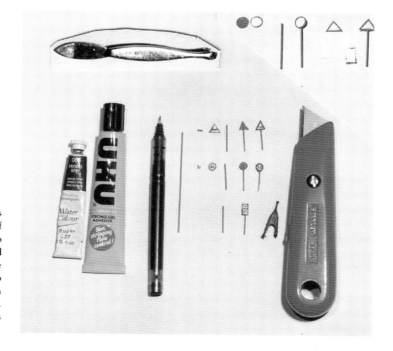

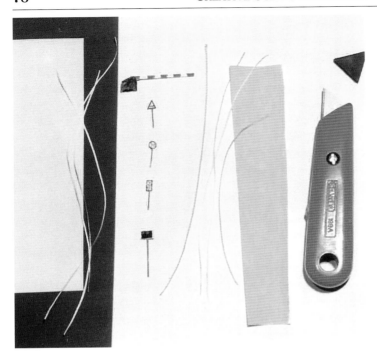

Left The range of road signs is further extended with crossing barriers and lights, and white and yellow lines. The barriers are double strips of white plastic card with red markings painted on. The lights are small pieces of painted cocktail stick stuck onto white plastic card with superimposed grey-painted paper. Thin strips of paper form the lines, some painted yellow.

Below The prototype at Harlech – the inset shows the crossing approach with yellow and white lines and warning sign.

Right The completed model.

Boats

Again, my boat-building is now in 2mm scale, though of course exactly the same method is applicable in 4mm or larger, and would in fact be easier, although perhaps more detailing would be required to look really effective (such as buckets, barrels, fishing gear, etc).

I made all the boats you see on my layouts in the way described here. This is the quayside on 'Caer Faban'.

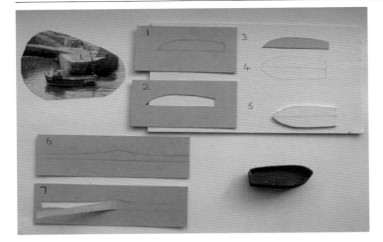

Having taken or obtained photos of the sort of boats I want to model, I draw half a basic water-line section of each boat on cereal packet card (1), cut it out (2 and 3), put the template on mount board, draw that half, then turn it over and draw a mirror-image (4), then cut out the whole piece (5). That way I ensure that I get a symmetrical shape! Then I draw the sides (6), cut one half out and turn it over to make sure it's the same (7), mark and cut that, then stick it to the former and paint it. If it goes wrong, I just start again till I've got it right – card is cheap!

To make a collection of boats, I cut out several templates that can be used again. These examples include the rowing boats for 'Porth Kernow'.

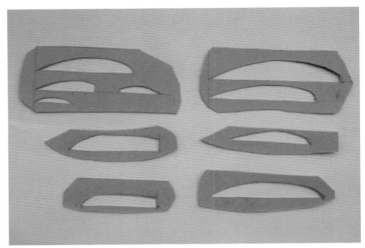

The basic hulls for the boats on 'Porth Kernow'.

I then construct cabins or other superstructures from thin card or plastic card, paint them and the hull, and add details such as masts, wires, chains, decking and boards. The second view shows some finished boats at the quayside.

Above For bigger boats I may need to make a bigger deck former just slightly larger than the 'water-line' one. Perhaps my biggest challenge was the special coastal ship on the slipway at Husum on my 'Der Nordseehafen' layout, where I had to make the whole hull, but this I also did with cereal packet card following the same basic technique. Here is the finished harbour scene.

Below A couple of finished boats at the quayside on 'Clogwyn'.

7
CAMEO SCENES

In this chapter I will concentrate on views of some of my best cameo scenes, because I think they typify my approach to modelling, and are the best way of convincing you that this kind of small-scale scene can be made effective without too much skill – mainly time, patience, and a desire to be creative, which is really the theme of this whole book.

Take, for example, the 'Wild West' town on 'Rocky Ridge', shown in the accompanying photograph. In essence this is a few simple houses constructed as described in Chapter 4, but they are set on a hillside on each side of a road. There

are a few extra details: a couple of water tanks on the roofs (made like the culvert pipe in Chapter 6, but set vertically), cotton-wool smoke coming out of a chimney, and added proprietary items such as telegraph poles, cars, trees and figures. It's not really anything special, but in the context of the whole scene I hope you'll agree that it looks in place – it's not too big, but conveys the atmosphere of the place in its setting.

Another example of a small town is the one on my 'Shelby's Landing' layout. This was in fact the first time I had modelled an American scene, working as always from photographs of suitable

The 'Wild West' town on 'Rocky Ridge'.

Above A small town on 'Shelby's Landing'.

Below The mine on 'High Peaks Railroad'.

The harbour on 'North West Valley Lines'.

prototypes and/or models. Unlike the 'Rocky Ridge' version, each of these buildings is quite different, reflecting the character of the small town on the Eastern seaboard. In spite of the variety, they are all made from mount board, cereal packet card, paper and plastic card with Downesglaze windows, using the methods described in Chapter 4.

Moving on to industrial complexes, you might argue that there is more scope for this in the States, and it was the enormous potential in scenic terms that drew me to American subjects. However, I'm sure that there are similar clusters of old buildings in Britain, or indeed most other countries. As always, it's mainly a question of positioning them in a suitable environment.

The mine buildings on 'High Peaks Railroad' are set in a dip with rock faces around them and a harbour with gravel loader in front. I concede that having two levels of tracks here would stretch the credibility of a British scene, but otherwise there's no reason why it should not work equally well. On each of my layouts I have two or three 'focal points', which have a greater concentration of structures, that draw the observer's eye.

Also on 'High Peaks Railroad' and 'North West Valley Lines' I made use of gravel loaders to create interesting subjects, while trying to ensure that they did not over-dominate and detract from the evocative atmosphere of the whole scene.

'Caer Faban'

I've made lots of models of individual buildings from prototypes, but only once an accurate replica of a whole farm on a detachable board, so I could later make a present of it to the owners, our friends John and Margaret Begley. However, so that they didn't have to wait too long, I also made a replica to fix permanently on my layout. I therefore thought I would focus on this as an example of my detailing techniques. It is certainly my most realistic representation of a place, and over which I took even more time and effort than usual.

I started by taking photographs of my intended subject, on this occasion from all sides, and worked out how much I could represent on my

The actual Caer Faban Farm.

hillside while allowing for realistic surroundings that, while not strictly prototypical, were still characteristic of Snowdonia. I found that there was room for the farmhouse, barns and yard, together with a somewhat reduced garden at the front, vegetable plot at the side, and parts of two fields behind.

I cut out a piece of plywood and stuck pieces of mount board on the sides and back, shaped to the contours of the hillside I wished to create. I then stuck on formers of mount board and strips of card to make the rising ground behind and to the right of the farmhouse, covered it with the usual pieces of moist sheet impregnated with PVA. Where necessary I used small amounts of 'Sculptamold' to shape the other bits of land that were not absolutely flat.

The stream bed was formed at this stage, partly by cutting a deep groove in the plywood.

The farmyard tarmac was a piece of wet and dry paper painted light grey and 'worn' by rubbing with a wet finger.

The buildings were drawn to scale on mount board as usual, doors and windows cut out and the walls, where appropriate, faced with stone and brick Plastikard or similar, but on the farmhouse and one or two other walls the rendering was represented by fine sandpaper.

The glazing for some of the small windows was Downesglaze, but for most I used clear plastic and made my own frames with Slater's microstrip. The porch, greenhouse and conservatory glass and frames were also made in this way. The conservatory roof was a piece of shaped Plastikard painted black.

The roofs of the buildings were cereal packet card faced with slate Plastikard, the chimneys were mount board faced with brick Plastikard, the pots were made from Slater's plastic rodding, the doors were card or Plastikard, some corrugated, as was the shed roof. The barge boards were cereal packet card painted green.

The fields were dyed lint, with other patches of grass made from Heki 'Grasfaser' or small pieces of grass matting, notably in front of the farmhouse.

The vegetable plot and muddy areas were made with frame sealant. The hedges were strips of green kitchen scourer brushed with PVA and

Two views of the first version of 'Caer Faban'.

'Pelican Creek'
('N', American outline, 2001)

Set in the southern Rockies, this was based on photos from 'Pelican Bay' (Paul Scoles, *Model Railroad Planning*, 2000) and 'Leigh Creek' (Geoff Nott, *Great Model Railroads*, 2000). (*Continental Modeller*, August 2001)

The gravel loader on 'Pelican Creek'.

The canyon on 'Pelican Creek'.

'High Peaks Railroad'
('N', American outline, 2002)

Inspired by 'Catford Creek and Bear Mountain' (*Continental Modeller*, 1998), 'Dolly Varden Mines' (*Model Railroader*, March 1997), and a sawmill (*Narrow Gauge and Shortline Gazette*, 2001). (*Continental Modeller*, August 2002)

General views of 'High Peaks Railroad'.

Above Logging operations on 'High Peaks Railroad'.

Below A close-up of the logging shed.

North West Valley Lines
('N', American outline, 2003)

Set in the Pacific North West, based on photos from magazines.
(*Continental Modeller*, August 2003)

Above An aerial view of 'North West Valley Lines'.

Below A closer view of the gravel loader on the harbour.

Above Gravel operations on 'North West Valley Lines'.

Below The layout's small trestle bridge.

'Rocky Ridge'
('N', American outline, 2004)

Set in Colorado, partly inspired by 'HO Chamatiago and Southern' (*Narrow Gauge and Shortline Gazette*, 2002). The name is the one my wife gave to the steep hillside opposite the old cottage 'Clogwyn' near Beddgelert. (*Continental Modeller*, August 2004)

Above The town, hills and canyon on 'Rocky Ridge'.

Below Looking across the layout towards the 'Wild West' town.

The town in its mountain setting.

Above A close-up of the centre top line on 'Rocky Ridge'.

Below A close-up of the rocks and stream on the layout.

'Dyffryn' (2nd version) ('N', 2004)

The first 'N' gauge 'Dyffryn' layout of 1998 depicted a typical North Wales valley ('dyffryn' is the northern equivalent of 'cwm' – 'valley' – in Welsh), although the river scene was inspired by that on Richard Coy's 'Porkington' layout. The baseboard was in two sections that were badly joined, so it couldn't really be transported and exhibited.

The second version was based on the upper Conwy Valley (River Lledr), featuring Roman Bridge station and the ruined castle and houses at Dolwyddelan, as well as 'Las Ynys', the restored house of the famous 'sleeping bard' near Harlech, and also a house from Beddgelert. (*Railway Modeller*, December 2004)

Above A general view of the 'Dyffryn' layout.

Below The left-hand end of the layout.

The ruined castle on 'Dyffryn' was based on that at Dolwyddelan.

Above The station and signal box on 'Dyffryn'.

Below A closer view of the station, based on the prototype at Roman Bridge.

Above A model of the home of Ellis Wynne (Y Bardd Cwsc) on the 'Dyffryn' layout.

Below Another model based on a prototype: the house from Beddgelert.

'Clogwyn'
('N', 2005)

Named after the hill farm cottage near Beddgelert, where four generations of our family have spent holidays, this layout also features the Plas Café and station at Harlech, and the quayside at Barmouth. (*Railway Modeller*, November 2005)

Above A view of the right-hand side of the 'Clogwyn' layout.

Below A passenger train on the left-hand side of the layout.

Another general view of the 'Clogwyn' layout.

Above The quayside on 'Clogwyn'.

Below Harlech station in model form on the 'Clogwyn' layout.

'Caer Faban'
('N', 2006)

Named after the farm near Llanrwst where our friends the Begleys live, it is modelled authentically. It also included a model of the toll bridge and house at Penmaenpool near Dolgellau, with an estuary based partly on the Aber and partly on the Glaslyn at Porthmadog. (*Railway Modeller*, October 2006)

Above The toll-bridge and house (and station halt) on the 'Caer Faban' layout were based on Penmaenpool near Dolgellau.

Below Detail on the 'Caer Faban' layout.

'Cobra Canyon'
('N', American outline, 2007)

This is a general canyon scene loosely set in the Rocky Mountains, with a mine building inspired by Russ Lucas's 'Nebraska and Platte Railroad' (*Narrow Gauge and Shortline Gazette*, March/April 2006), and logging buildings from Bob Hazard's 'Crabbit and Pitchahissee Railroad' (*Model Railroader*, April 2006). (*Continental Modeller*, June 2007)

Above A close-up of the mine on 'Cobra Canyon'.

Below The right-hand side of the layout.

Above A general view of 'Cobra Canyon'.

'Die alte Mühle'
('N', German outline, 2007)

A recreation of a north German landscape, the station was modelled on that at Husum in Schleswig Holstein, with the river and mill from Westermühlen some 20 miles to the south near the Kiel Canal. My favourite German poet Theodor Storm lived in Husum, and his grandfather was the miller at Westermühlen. I have modelled the latter in its restored state. (*Continental Modeller*, April 2008)

Above A view of the 'Die alte Mühle' layout looking from left to right.

Right The layout looking from right to left.

A closer view of the riverside area.

Above An ICE train rounds the curve on 'Die alte Mühle'.

Below A view across the centre of the layout.

The station and river on the 'Die alte Mühle' layout.

Above Another view across the left-hand side of 'Die alte Mühle'.

Below A smaller version of Husum station featured on the 'Die alte Mühle' layout.

An ICE train approaches the level crossing on 'Die alte Mühle', in views showing the two reed-thatched cottages.

Above A close-up of one of the thatched cottages.

Below The farm on 'Die alte Mühle'.

Above The ruined barn on 'Die alte Mühle'.

Below The old mill.

'Der Nordseehafen'
('N', German outline, 2008)

A second module built as an extension to 'Die alte Mühle', this layout can also be operated separately, with a necessarily reduced version of the harbour and quayside at Husum, and a section of the low-lying grazing land of the area. (*Continental Modeller*, July 2009)

Above The left-hand end of the 'Der Nordseehafen' layout.

Below The centre of the layout.

The right-hand end of the 'Der Nordseehafen' layout.

Above The quayside on 'Der Nordseehafen'.

Below The level crossing on the layout.

Above A thatched house on the 'Der Nordseehafen' layout.

Below Low-lying fields on 'Der Nordseehafen'.

'Porth Kernow'
('N', 2009)

This Cornish estuary and quayside layout features a viaduct and buildings based on Polperro prototypes. (Scheduled for publication in *Railway Modeller*)

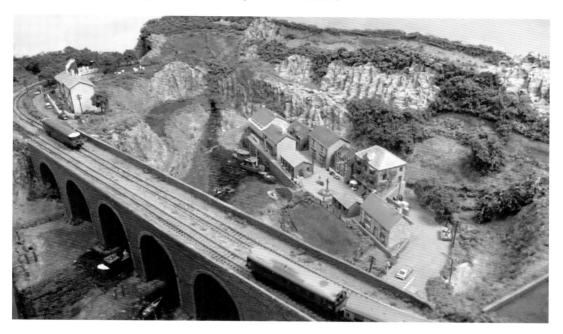

Above Trains meet on the viaduct at 'Porth Kernow'.

Below A closer view of the railcar on the viaduct.

Above The viaduct crossing the estuary on 'Porth Kernow', with the fishing village beyond.

Below The quayside on 'Porth Kernow'.

Above A closer look at the quayside.

Below The houses by the railway line.

Above An assortment of buildings on the quayside on 'Porth Kernow'.

Below The level crossing in its sylvan setting. The trees are from 'The Model Tree Shop'.

LIST OF ARTICLES BY THE AUTHOR IN THE RAILWAY PRESS

Model Railway Enthusiast

1995 June   'Bodarfryn': 'OO' layout article with scenic details and ideas.

Dec   'Harlech': 'OO' layout article with scenery and structure description.

1997 Jan   'Dorothea': 'OO' layout article with scenery and structure description.

July   'Rivers, Rocks, Plots and Quarries: article on 'OO' scenery.

Dec   'The Cambrian Connection': 'OO' layout article with scenery description.

1998 May   'The House at Penhelig': constructing a house in 'N' gauge.

June   'Dyffryn': 'N' gauge layout article showing scenery construction.

July   'Card Cradle for Plastic Roof Assembly': modelling tip.

Aug   'A Home-Made Jig for Cutting Track': modelling tip.

Oct   'Flowing Water': modelling tip (bath sealant).

Nov   'Varnish Water': modelling tip.

Dec   'Heather Root Trees': modelling tip.

1999 Jan   'Plumber's Hemp Grass': modelling tip.

Feb   'Brush Bristle Flowers': modelling tip.

Mar   'Rocks Cast in Plaster': modelling tip.

Apr   'Plaster-Soaked Ground Cover': modelling tip.

Jun-Sept   'Cambrington': 'N' gauge layout article in four parts.

Model Railway Collector

1999 Dec   'Culvert Pipes': modelling construction.

2000 Jun   'The 3-D Effect': making scenery backgrounds.

'Scratchbuilding Road Signs': modelling construction in 'N'.

July   'Lasynys': scratchbuilding a house in 2mm scale.

Continental Modeller

2000 Aug   'Shelby's Landing': layout article, American 'N' gauge.

2001 Aug   'Pelican Creek': layout article, American 'N' gauge.

2002 Aug   'High Peaks Railroad': layout article, American 'N' gauge.

Oct   'Disappearing Tracks': modelling tip.

2003 Aug   'North West Valley Lines': layout article, American 'N' gauge.

2004 Aug   'Rocky Ridge': layout article, American 'N' gauge.

2005 Mar   'Building Trestles': modelling tip, American 'N' gauge.

2007 Jun   'Cobra Canyon': layout article, American 'N' gauge.

2008 Apr   'Die Alte Mühle': layout article, German 'N' gauge.

2009 July   'Der Nordseehafen': layout article, German 'N' gauge.

N Scale Railroading

2001 July/Aug   'Shelby's Landing': layout article, American 'N' gauge.

2003 Mar/Apr   'Pelican Creek': layout article, American 'N' gauge.

Railway Modeller

2004 Dec   'Dyffryn': layout article, British 'N' gauge.

2005 Nov   'Clogwyn': layout article, British 'N' gauge.

2006 Oct   'Caer Faban': layout article, British 'N' gauge.

2010 July   'Porth Kernow': layout article, British 'N' gauge.

N-Scale Magazine

2005 Sept/Oct   'Rocky Ridge': layout article, American 'N' gauge.

2006 Jan/Feb   'North West Valley Lines': layout article, American 'N' gauge.

2010 May/June   'Dyffryn': layout article, British 'N' gauge

N-Bahn-Magazin

2010 Summer   'Die Alte Mühle': layout article, German 'N' gauge.

INDEX